Student
Leadership
Practices
Inventory

STUDENT WORKBOOK
SECOND EDITION

James M. Kouzes
Barry Z. Posner, Ph.D.

JOSSEY-BASS
A Wiley Imprint
www.josseybass.com

ISBN: 0-7879-8019-6

Published by Jossey-Bass
A Wiley Imprint
989 Market Street, San Francisco, CA 94103-1741   www.josseybass.com

Readers should be aware that Internet websites offered as citations and/or sources for further information may have changed or disappeared between the time this was written and when it is read.

Jossey-Bass books and products are available through most bookstores. To contact Jossey-Bass directly call our Customer Care Department within the U.S. at 800-956-7739, outside the U.S. at 317-572-3986, or fax 317-572-4002.

Jossey-Bass also publishes its books in a variety of electronic formats. Some content that appears in print may not be available in electronic books.

Printed in the United States of America
SECOND EDITION

PB Printing   10 9 8

CONTENTS

People WHO BECOME

leaders

DON'T *always* **seek**

THE challenges

THEY **Face.**

CHALLENGES

also SEEK leaders.

1   Leadership: What People Do When They're Leading

Leadership is everyone's business. That's the conclusion we have come to after over two decades of research into the behaviors and actions of people who are making a difference in organizations, clubs, teams, classes, schools, campuses, communities, and even in their families. We found that leadership is an observable, learnable set of practices.

Contrary to some myths, leadership is not a mystical and ethereal process that cannot be understood by ordinary people. Given the opportunity for feedback and practice, those with the desire and persistence to lead—to make a difference—can substantially improve their ability to do so.

The *Leadership Practices Inventory (LPI)* is part of an extensive research project into the everyday actions and behaviors of people, at all levels and across a variety of settings, as they are leading. Through our research we identified The Five Practices of Exemplary Leadership® that are common to all leadership experiences.* In collaboration with others, we extended our original findings to student leaders and to school and college environments and created the student version of the *LPI*.

The *Student LPI* is a tool, not a test, designed to assess your current leadership skills. It will identify your areas of strength as well as areas of leadership that need to be further developed.

The *Student LPI* helps you discover the extent to which you (in your role as a leader of a student group or organization) engage in the following Five Practices of Exemplary Leaders:

Model the Way

Leaders are clear about their personal values and beliefs. They keep people and projects on course by behaving consistently with these values and setting

---

*For more information on our original work, see *The Leadership Challenge* (3rd ed.) (Jossey-Bass, 2002).

an example for how they expect others to act. By focusing on key priorities, they make it easier for others to achieve goals.

The commitments of leaders to Model the Way involve

- **Finding your voice** by clarifying your personal values
- **Setting the example** by aligning actions with shared values

While Jason Hegland was the captain of his water polo team, he learned the hard way about how to be the team leader: "First, I was just plain bossy. I was also stubborn. Things were supposed to go *my* way. Worst of all, I didn't show anyone else what they meant to the team as a whole. I cut people down when I should have built them up." Luckily, early in the season, a teammate brought these flaws to his attention, and, to his credit, Jason reflected on what was really important and quickly made changes, in his words, "to show everyone how a real captain acts."

One of the first things he did was to get himself to school every day at 5:00 A.M. for practice. When he saw other players during the day, he would ask them why they weren't at practice. Soon enough, Jason said, "The message about practices sunk in and we had 100 percent attendance." He also opened up communications. Every day he asked his teammates: "What didn't we do well yesterday that we need to work on today?" He asked those who were better players than he was what he needed to do to improve himself. Furthermore, Jason stopped focusing on errors and became the "head cheerleader" for the team, mentioning at each postgame meeting at least one good thing that each of his teammates had done.

As for results, Jason pointed out that, while the changes he made in his leadership style didn't lead his team to the state championship, it was the first time that any school from a Chicago suburb placed within the top ten, and most importantly, he said, "That year the team members were the closest that they had ever been to one another." The lesson for Jason: "I learned that those who follow you are only as good as the model you present them with."

Inspire a Shared Vision

Leaders look toward and beyond the horizon. They envision the future with a positive and hopeful outlook. Leaders are expressive and attract other people to their organizations and teams through their genuineness. They communicate and show others how their interests can be met through commitment to a common purpose.

The commitments of leaders to Inspire a Shared Vision involve

- **Envisioning the future** by imagining exciting and ennobling possibilities
- **Enlisting others in a common vision** by appealing to shared aspirations

The insight for Filip Morovich was learning that "leadership is not about being the great heroic solver of all problems; it is about inspiring people to believe that the problem can be solved by working together." In one of Filip's courses, the assignment was to produce a one-hour musical play (with singing, dancing, and all the rest!). Pretty much everyone in the class was afraid and daunted by this task because few of them had any theater experience or particular acting talents. Filip described the scene: "The group was adrift and everyone was sitting around staring at one another in stark silence. I got very angry inside, and at that instant I had a vision. A real flash of lightning in my mind made it clear to me that we could be successful. But at this point it was only my idea, only my flash of inspiration, and so I had to share it and make it a common belief among us all."

He decided some drama was necessary to get everyone's attention, so he picked up his pen, raised it high in the air, and dropped it onto the binder on his lap. A bomb going off in the room could not have been louder. This had the intended effect and Filip launched into inspiring a shared vision: "I used a hopeful and positive tone of voice. I was excited and called on our collective strength as a team to move forward and be successful. I hoped that my excitement and positive mood would prove infectious and revitalize the group. We all noticed an uplift of our mood and we could literally see a sparkle of hope returning to one another's eyes. The key was making the vision of our success a joint process because we all came to believe that we could do this."

Challenge the Process

Leaders are pioneers—people who seek out new opportunities and are willing to change the status quo. They innovate, experiment, and explore ways to improve the organization. They treat mistakes as learning experiences. Leaders also stay prepared to meet whatever challenges may confront them. They plan projects and break them down into achievable steps, creating opportunities for small wins.

The commitments of leaders to Challenge the Process involve

- **Searching for opportunities** by seeking innovative ways to change, grow, and improve
- **Experimenting and taking risks** by constantly generating small wins and learning from mistakes

Allison Avon told us that the idea of Challenging the Process took on real meaning for her when she was in charge of her school's annual Charity Fashion Show. The school typically raised funds to buy toys for the children at a local Head Start program. For various reasons the program administrators didn't want the school to buy the children toys, and "we couldn't convince them otherwise." Everyone was pretty discouraged and wanted to cancel the fashion show.

Allison wasn't ready to give up, so she asked everyone for their ideas and what alternatives they could imagine. As a result they decided, "Perhaps if we bought the children educational items such as books instead of toys, then maybe the Head Start program administrators would be more receptive." In the end the fashion show and their day with the children—sharing and reading books together—were great successes. As Allison reported: "The results were better than we could have hoped for. This process of trial and error gave me a new perspective on what is required of a successful leader. When the process challenges you," Allison retorts, "challenge back."

Enable Others to Act

Leaders infuse people with energy and confidence, developing relationships based on mutual trust. They stress collaborative goals. They actively involve others in planning, giving them sufficient discretion to make their own decisions. Leaders ensure that people feel strong and capable.

The commitments leaders make to Enable Others to Act involve

- **Fostering collaboration** by promoting cooperative goals and building trust
- **Strengthening others** by sharing power and discretion

With beads of sweat dripping down his face, Peter Freeman continued to attack the nails with his hammer. It was a blazing hot day in Harlan, Kentucky, and he and his classmates had to finish the roof by the end of the week; but it was already Thursday and the roof was not close to being finished. "As I looked around," said Peter, "I saw a group of kids who were unmotivated, tired, and hot." He began nailing again, thinking to himself, "We have got to finish this roof." He looked up again and saw another possibility: a group of highly motivated, energetic people who would work together to accomplish the task. It began to dawn on Peter that "merely working hard on my own would not allow us to reach the goal of finishing the roof in another day."

So he set out to enable those around him, reminding them of the purpose and urgency of their task and how important it was for them to work together as a team. "This brought about an amazing change," he reported, and "rejuvenated and reenergized, my friends attacked their work with vigor." Peter realized that he could not accomplish "my goals on my own without the help of a team." The key was to involve others in making key decisions and sharing ideas about how to best accomplish "OUR" goal. "I asked for their opinions," Peter explained, "finding out from them what they thought was the best way to go about things." In fact, before he realized it, others got excited and took on new responsibilities, making choices and acting like leaders themselves . . . and the job was done!

Encourage the Heart

Leaders encourage people to persist in their efforts by linking recognition with accomplishments and visibly recognizing contributions to the common vision. They express pride in the achievements of the group, letting others know that their efforts are appreciated. Leaders also find ways to celebrate milestones. They nurture a team spirit, which enables people to sustain continued efforts.

The commitments of leaders to Encourage the Heart involve

- **Recognizing contributions** by showing appreciation for individual excellence
- **Celebrating the values and victories** by creating a spirit of community

"Being a leader on my volleyball team," Kirsten Cornell explained, "forced me to learn lessons about encouragement and put them into practice." One of her main goals was to create a positive atmosphere on the team: "So I made sure that I recognized people for making good plays with gestures as simple as high-fives and words of praise (and my teammates got in the habit of doing the same)." As Kirsten put it: "I found that encouraging my teammates was one of the easiest and most beneficial thing I could do to make the team better."

Kirsten said that part of creating an uplifting attitude on the team was letting the players know that she had confidence in them: "I showed my teammates with both words and actions that I believed in them. With words I would tell them that I knew they could make a perfect pass or get a great hit. With actions I showed them my belief in them in a tangible way by spreading out the sets between players so that everyone had a chance to get into the game." Also critical, she said, was "taking an honest interest in each player. I got to know my teammates as both people and athletes. I knew the things they were dealing with outside of the thirty-foot square where we met to play, and this allowed me to realize when they needed extra encouragement and support."

Finally, Kirsten created a culture of celebration by acknowledging accomplishments, however small they might have been, both on and off the court (for example, having birthday cards signed by everyone on the team). "This culture," she explained, "caused us to have fun while we worked and to take pride in what we achieved together."

Somewhere,

s o m e t i m e ,

THE *leader* **within**

EACH OF US

MAY **get**

THE CALL

to STEP forward.

2 Frequently Asked Questions About the *Student LPI*

Question 1: How reliable and valid is the Student LPI?

Answer: The question of reliability can be answered in two ways. First, the *Student LPI* has shown sound psychometric properties. The scale for each leadership practice is internally reliable, meaning that the statements within each practice are highly correlated with one another. Second, results of multivariate analyses indicate that the statements within each leadership practice are more highly correlated (or associated) with one another than they are between the five leadership practices.

In terms of validity (or, "So what difference do the scores make?"), the *Student LPI* has good face validity and predictive validity. This means, first, that the results make sense to people. Second, scores on the *Student LPI* significantly differentiate high-performing leaders from their less successful counterparts. Whether measured by the leader, his or her peers, or student personnel administrators, those student leaders who engage more frequently, rather than less frequently, in the five leadership practices are more effective.

Question 2: What are the right answers?

Answer: There are no universal right answers when it comes to leadership. The research indicates that the more frequently you are perceived as engaging in the behaviors and actions identified in the *Student LPI*, the more likely it is that you will be perceived as an effective leader. The higher your scores on the *Student LPI-Observer*, the more others will perceive you as, for example:

- Having personal credibility
- Being effective in running meetings
- Successfully representing your organization or group to nonmembers
- Generating a sense of enthusiasm and cooperation
- Having a high-performing team

Empirical findings show a strong and positive relationship between the extent to which people report their leaders engaging in this set of five leadership practices and how motivated, committed, and productive they themselves feel.

Question 3: Should my perceptions be consistent with the ratings other people give me?

Answer: Research indicates that trust in the leader is essential if other people (for example, fellow members of a group, team, or organization) are going to follow that person over time. People must experience the leader as believable, credible, and trustworthy. Trust—whether in a leader or any other person—is developed through consistency in behavior. Trust is further established when words and deeds are congruent.

This does not mean, however, that you will always be perceived in exactly the same way by every person in every situation. Some people may not see you as often as others do, and therefore they may rate you differently on the same behavior. Some people simply may not know you as well as others do. Also, you may appropriately behave differently in different situations, such as in a crisis versus during more stable times. Others may have different expectations of you, and still others may perceive the rating descriptions (such as "once in a while" or "fairly often") differently.

Therefore, the key issue is not whether your self-ratings and the ratings from others are exactly the same, but whether people perceive consistency between what you say you do and what you actually do. The only way you can know the answer to this question is to solicit feedback. The *Student LPI-Observer* has been designed for this purpose.

Research indicates that people tend to see themselves more positively than others do. The *Student LPI-Self* norms are consistent with this general trend; scores on the *Student LPI-Self* tend to be somewhat higher than scores on the *Student LPI-Observer*. *Student LPI* scores also tend to be higher than LPI scores of experienced managers and executives in the private and public sectors.

Question 4: Can I change my leadership behavior?

Answer: It is certainly possible—even for experienced people—to learn new skills. You will increase your chances of changing your behavior if you receive feedback on what level you have achieved with a particular skill, observe a positive model of that skill, set some improvement goals for yourself, practice the skill, ask for updated feedback on your performance, and then set new goals. The practices that are assessed with the *Student LPI* fall into the category of learnable skills.

But some things can be changed only if there is a strong and genuine inner desire to make a difference. For example, enthusiasm for a cause is unlikely to be developed through education or job assignments; it must come from within.

Use the information from the *Student LPI* to better understand how you currently behave as a leader, both from your own perspective and from the perspective of others. Note where there are consistencies and inconsistencies. Understand which leadership behaviors and practices you feel comfortable engaging in and those you feel uncomfortable with. Determine which leadership behaviors and practices you can improve on, and take steps to improve your leadership skills and confidence in leading other people and groups. The following sections will help you to become more effective in leadership.

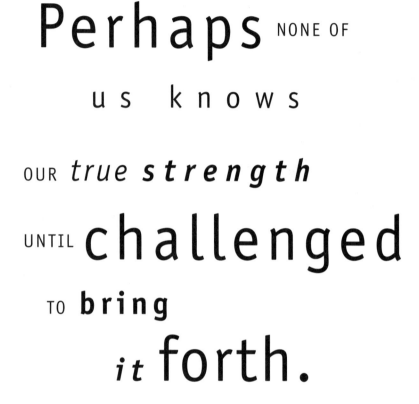

Perhaps NONE OF us knows OUR *true* **strength** UNTIL challenged TO **bring** *it* forth.

3 Recording Your Scores

On pages 15 through 17 are grids for recording your *Student LPI* scores. In the event that your instructor or facilitator had your scores centrally or computer scored, you may skip this chapter.

Each grid is for recording scores for the corresponding items for each of the five Leadership Practices from the *Student LPI-Self* and *Student LPI-Observer.* An abbreviated form of each item is printed beside the grid as a handy reference.

1. In the first column labeled "Self-Rating" on the Model the Way grid, write the scores that you gave yourself. The Model the Way grid is for recording scores to items 1, 6, 11, 16, 21, and 26 that pertain to finding your voice and setting an example. If others were asked to complete the *Student LPI-Observer* and if the forms were returned to you, enter their scores in the columns (A, B, C, D, E, and so on) under "Observers' Ratings." Simply transfer the numbers from page 4 of each *Student LPI-Observer* to your scoring grids, using one column for each observer. For example, enter the first observer's scores in column A, the second observer's scores in column B, and so on. The grids provide space for the scores of as many as ten observers.

2. After all scores have been entered, total each column in the row labeled "Totals."

3. Add all the totals for observers; do not include the "self" total. Write this grand total in the space marked "Total of All Observers' Scores." To obtain the average, divide the grand total by the number of people who completed the *Student LPI-Observer.* Write this average in the blank provided.

The following sample grid for Model the Way shows how the grid would look with scores for self and five observers entered.

Sample Grid with Scores from Self and Five Observers

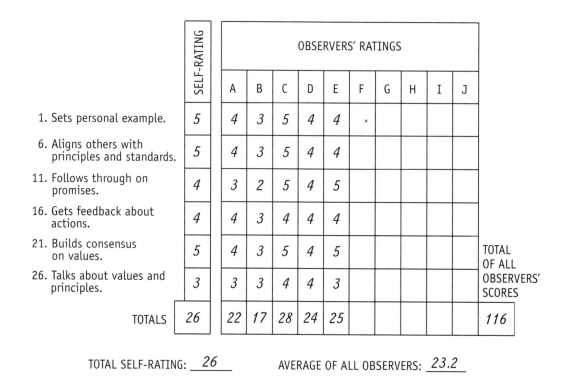

	SELF-RATING	OBSERVERS' RATINGS									
		A	B	C	D	E	F	G	H	I	J
1. Sets personal example.	5	4	3	5	4	4	.				
6. Aligns others with principles and standards.	5	4	3	5	4	4					
11. Follows through on promises.	4	3	2	5	4	5					
16. Gets feedback about actions.	4	4	3	4	4	4					
21. Builds consensus on values.	5	4	3	5	4	5					
26. Talks about values and principles.	3	3	3	4	4	3					
TOTALS	26	22	17	28	24	25					

TOTAL OF ALL OBSERVERS' SCORES: 116

TOTAL SELF-RATING: ___26___   AVERAGE OF ALL OBSERVERS: ___23.2___

Complete the next four blank grids in the same manner.

The Inspire a Shared Vision grid is for recording scores to items 2, 7, 12, 17, 22, and 27 that pertain to envisioning the future and enlisting the support of others.

The Challenge the Process grid is for recording scores to items 3, 8, 13, 18, 23, and 28 that pertain to searching for opportunities, experimenting, and taking risks.

The Enable Others to Act grid is for recording scores to items 4, 9, 14, 19, 24, and 29 that pertain to fostering collaboration and strengthening others.

The Encourage the Heart grid pertains to items 5, 10, 15, 20, 25, and 30 that pertain to recognizing contributions and celebrating values and victories.

As you look at individual scores, remember the rating system that was used:

"1" means that you *rarely or seldom* engage in the behavior.
"2" means that you engage in the behavior *once in a while*.
"3" means that you *sometimes* engage in the behavior.
"4" means that you engage in the behavior *often*.
"5" means that you engage in the behavior *very frequently or almost always*.

The next chapter will help you interpret your scores.

Model the Way

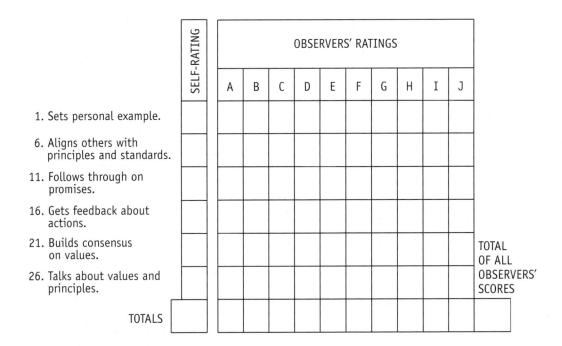

	SELF-RATING	OBSERVERS' RATINGS									
		A	B	C	D	E	F	G	H	I	J
1. Sets personal example.											
6. Aligns others with principles and standards.											
11. Follows through on promises.											
16. Gets feedback about actions.											
21. Builds consensus on values.											
26. Talks about values and principles.											
TOTALS											

TOTAL OF ALL OBSERVERS' SCORES

Inspire a Shared Vision

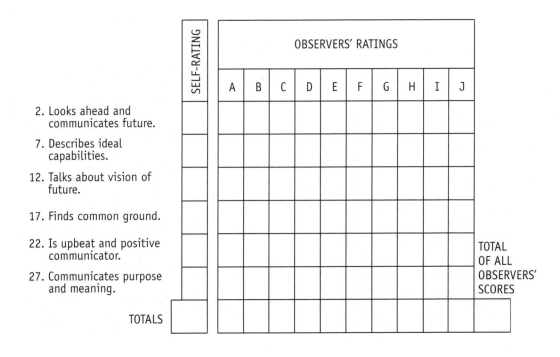

	SELF-RATING	OBSERVERS' RATINGS									
		A	B	C	D	E	F	G	H	I	J
2. Looks ahead and communicates future.											
7. Describes ideal capabilities.											
12. Talks about vision of future.											
17. Finds common ground.											
22. Is upbeat and positive communicator.											
27. Communicates purpose and meaning.											
TOTALS											

TOTAL OF ALL OBSERVERS' SCORES

Challenge the Process

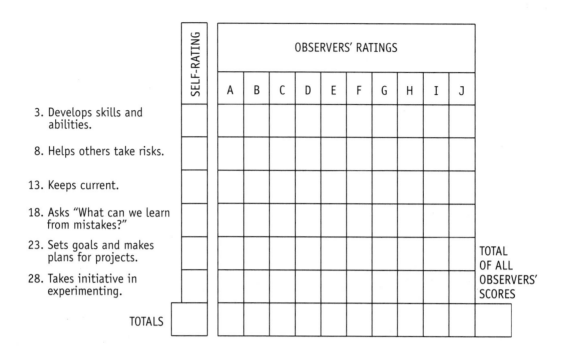

	SELF-RATING	OBSERVERS' RATINGS									
		A	B	C	D	E	F	G	H	I	J
3. Develops skills and abilities.											
8. Helps others take risks.											
13. Keeps current.											
18. Asks "What can we learn from mistakes?"											
23. Sets goals and makes plans for projects.											
28. Takes initiative in experimenting.											
TOTALS											

TOTAL OF ALL OBSERVERS' SCORES

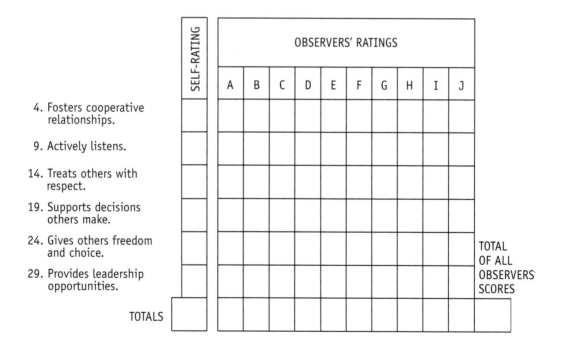 ## Enable Others to Act

	SELF-RATING	OBSERVERS' RATINGS									
		A	B	C	D	E	F	G	H	I	J
4. Fosters cooperative relationships.											
9. Actively listens.											
14. Treats others with respect.											
19. Supports decisions others make.											
24. Gives others freedom and choice.											
29. Provides leadership opportunities.											
TOTALS											

TOTAL OF ALL OBSERVERS' SCORES

Encourage the Heart

	SELF-RATING	OBSERVERS' RATINGS									
		A	B	C	D	E	F	G	H	I	J
5. Praises people.											
10. Encourages others.											
15. Provides support and appreciation.											
20. Publicly recognizes alignment with values.											
25. Celebrates accomplishments.											
30. Creatively recognizes people.											
TOTALS											

TOTAL OF ALL OBSERVERS SCORES

THE **unique** ROLE

OF **l e a d e r s**

IS TO *take us*

TO **places**

WE'VE **never**

been **before.**

4 Interpreting Your Scores

This section will help you to interpret your scores by looking at them in several ways and making notes to yourself about what you can do to become a more effective leader.

Ranking Your Ratings

Refer to Chapter Three, "Recording Your Scores." On each grid, look at your scores in the blanks marked "Total Self-Rating." Each of these totals represents your responses to the six statements about one of the five leadership practices. Each of your totals can range from a low of 6 to a high of 30.

In the chart that follows, write "1" to the left of the leadership practice with the highest total self-rating, "2" by the next-highest total self-rating, and so on. This ranking represents the leadership practices with which you feel most comfortable, second-most comfortable, and so on. The practice you identify with a "5" is the practice with which you feel least comfortable.

Again refer to the previous chapter, but this time look at your scores in the blanks marked "Average of All Observers." The number in each blank is the average score given to you by the people you asked to complete the *Student LPI-Observer.* Like each of your total self-ratings, this number can range from 6 to 30.

In the chart that follows, write "1" to the right of the leadership practice with the highest score, "2" by the next-highest score, and so on. This ranking represents the leadership practices that others feel you use most often, second-most often, and so on.

Self		Observers
_____	Model the Way	_____
_____	Inspire a Shared Vision	_____
_____	Challenge the Process	_____
_____	Enable Others to Act	_____
_____	Encourage the Heart	_____

Comparing Your Self-Ratings to Observers' Ratings

To compare your *Student LPI-Self* and *Student LPI-Observer* assessments, refer to the "Chart for Graphing Your Scores" on the next page. On the chart, designate your scores on the five leadership practices (Model, Inspire, Challenge, Enable, and Encourage) by marking each of these points with a capital "S" (for "Self"). Connect the five resulting "S scores" with a *solid line* and label the end of this line "Self" (see sample chart below).

If other people provided input through the *Student LPI-Observer,* designate the average observer scores (see the blanks labeled "Average of All Observers" on the scoring grids) by marking each of the points with a capital "O" (for "Observer"). Then connect the five resulting "O scores" with a *dashed line* and label the end of this line "Observer" (see sample chart). Completing this process will provide you with a graphic representation (one solid and one dashed line) illustrating the relationship between your self-perception and the observations of other people.

Sample Chart for Graphing Your Scores

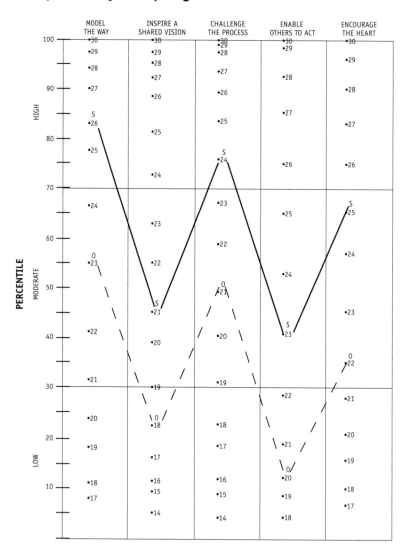

Chart for Graphing Your Scores

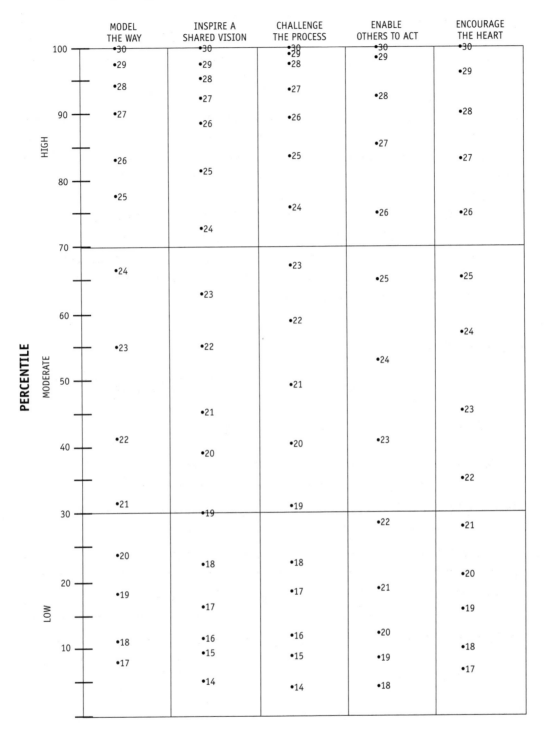

Percentile Scores

Look again at the "Chart for Graphing Your Scores." The column to the far left represents the *Student LPI-Self* percentile rankings for more than 2,200 student leaders. A percentile ranking is determined by the percentage of people who score at or below a given number. For example, if your total self-rating for Model the Way is at the 60th percentile line on the "Chart for Graphing Your Scores," this means that you assessed yourself higher than 60 percent of all people who have completed the *Student LPI;* you would be in the top 40 percent in this leadership practice. Studies indicate that a "high" score is one at or above the 70th percentile, a "low" score is one at or below the 30th percentile, and a score that falls between those ranges is considered "moderate."

Using these criteria, circle "H" (for "High"), "M" (for "Moderate"), or "L" (for "Low") for each leadership practice on the "Range of Scores" table below. Compared to other student leaders, where do your leadership practices tend to fall? (Given a "normal distribution," it is expected that most people's scores will fall within the moderate range.)

Range of Scores

IN MY PERCEPTION			IN OTHERS' PERCEPTION		
PRACTICE	RATING		PRACTICE	RATING	
Model the Way	H M L		Model the Way	H M L	
Inspire a Shared Vision	H M L		Inspire a Shared Vision	H M L	
Challenge the Process	H M L		Challenge the Process	H M L	
Enable Others to Act	H M L		Enable Others to Act	H M L	
Encourage the Heart	H M L		Encourage the Heart	H M L	

Exploring Specific Behaviors Within Leadership Practices

Looking at your scoring grids in Chapter Three, review each of the six behaviors on the *Student LPI* by leadership practice. One or two of the six behaviors within each leadership practice may be higher or lower than the rest. If so, on which specific statement is there variation? What do these differences suggest about becoming a better leader? Please write your thoughts in the following space.

 Model the Way

_____

_____

_____

_____

_____

_____

 Inspire a Shared Vision

_____

_____

_____

_____

_____

_____

_____

Challenge the Process

_____

_____

_____

_____

_____

Enable Others to Act

_____

_____

_____

_____

_____

Encourage the Heart

_____

_____

_____

_____

_____

Comparing Observers' Responses

Study the *Student LPI-Observer* scores for each of the five leadership practices. Consider both the practices and the specific behaviors associated with each one. In general, are the scores from your Observers most similar or different? On which leadership practices do the respondents agree? On which practices do they disagree? Where there are disagreements, is this across every behavior or just a few? Are there one (or two) respondents whose scores differ from the others? If your behavior is basically the same with all the people who assessed you, how do you explain the difference in ratings? Please write your thoughts in the following space.

Wanting TO LEAD AND
believing THAT
YOU *can* **lead** ARE THE
departure POINTS
ON THE PATH TO **leadership.**

LEADERSHIP IS AN ART—

A *performing* art—

AND THE **instrument**

IS THE **self.**

5 Summary and Action-Planning Worksheets

Take a few moments to summarize your *Student LPI* feedback by completing the following Strengths and Opportunities Summary Worksheet. Refer to the "Chart for Graphing Your Scores," the "Range of Scores" table, and any notes you have made.

After the summary worksheet you will find some suggestions for getting started on meeting the leadership challenge. With these suggestions in mind, review your *Student LPI* feedback and decide on the actions you will take to become an even more effective leader. Then complete the Action-Planning Worksheet to spell out the steps you will take. (One Action-Planning Worksheet is included in this workbook, but you may want to develop action plans for several practices or behaviors. You could make copies of the blank form before you fill it in or just use a separate sheet of paper for each leadership practice in which you plan to improve.)

Strengths and Opportunities Summary Worksheet

Strengths

Which of the leadership practices and behaviors are you most comfortable with? Why? Can you do more?

_____

_____

_____

_____

_____

_____

Areas for Improvement

What can you do to use a practice more frequently? What will it take to feel more comfortable doing so?

_____

_____

_____

_____

_____

_____

Following are ten suggestions for getting started on meeting the leadership challenge.

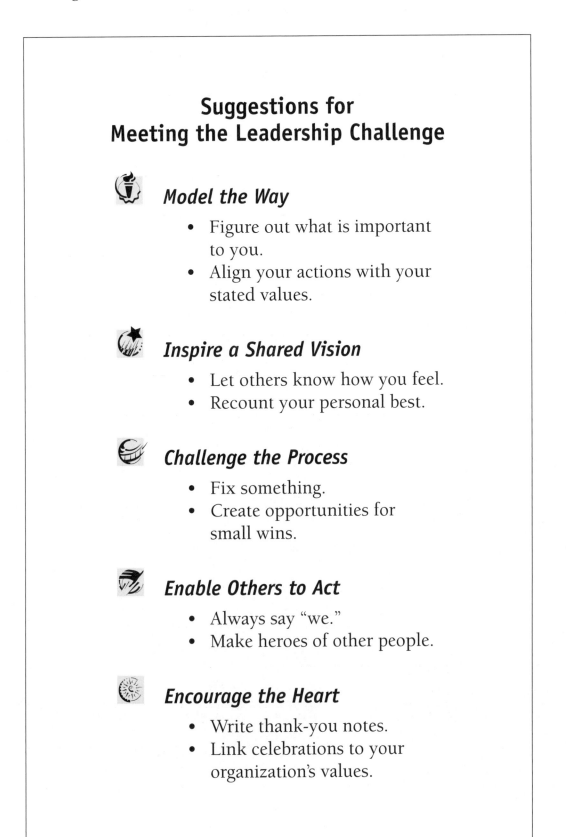

Suggestions for Meeting the Leadership Challenge

Model the Way

- Figure out what is important to you.
- Align your actions with your stated values.

Inspire a Shared Vision

- Let others know how you feel.
- Recount your personal best.

Challenge the Process

- Fix something.
- Create opportunities for small wins.

Enable Others to Act

- Always say "we."
- Make heroes of other people.

Encourage the Heart

- Write thank-you notes.
- Link celebrations to your organization's values.

Action-Planning Worksheet

1. What would you like to be better able to do?

   _____

   _____

   _____

   _____

   _____

   _____

   _____

   _____

2. What specific actions will you take?

   _____

   _____

   _____

   _____

   _____

   _____

   _____

   _____

3. What is the *first* action you will take? Who will be involved? When will you begin?

Action _____

_____

_____

People Involved _____

_____

_____

Target Date _____

_____

4. Complete this sentence: "I will know I have improved in this leadership skill when . . ."

_____

_____

_____

_____

5. When will you review your progress? _____

About the Authors

James M. Kouzes and *Barry Z. Posner* are the authors of the award-winning and best-selling book *The Leadership Challenge*. In addition, they have coauthored a number of other books on leadership, including *Credibility: How Leaders Gain It and Lose It, Why People Demand It*—chosen by *Industry Week* as one of the year's five best management books—as well as *Encouraging the Heart* and *The Academic Administrator's Guide to Exemplary Leadership*. Kouzes and Posner also developed the highly acclaimed *Leadership Practices Inventory (LPI)*, a 360-degree questionnaire assessing leadership behavior. The *LPI* is one of the most widely used leadership assessment instruments in the world. More than 300 doctoral dissertations and academic research projects have been based on The Five Practices of Exemplary Leadership® model.

Kouzes and Posner were named by the International Management Council as the 2001 recipients of the prestigious Wilbur M. McFeely Award. This honor puts them in the company of Ken Blanchard, Stephen Covey, Peter Drucker, Edward Deming, Francis Hesselbein, Lee Iacocca, Rosabeth Moss Kanter, Norman Vincent Peale, and Tom Peters, previous recipients of the award. In the book *Coaching for Leadership*, they were listed among the nation's top leadership educators. Kouzes and Posner are frequent conference speakers, and each has conducted leadership development programs for hundreds of organizations around the globe, including Alcoa, Applied Materials, AT&T, Australia Post, Bank of America, Bose, Charles Schwab, Cisco Systems, Community Leadership Association, Conference Board of Canada, Consumers Energy, Dell Computer, Deloitte & Touche, Egon Zehnder International, FedEx, Gymboree, Hewlett-Packard, IBM, JobsDB-Singapore, Johnson & Johnson, Kaiser Foundation Health Plans and Hospitals, Lawrence Livermore National Laboratory, L.L. Bean, 3M, Merck, Motorola, Network Appliance, Northrop Grumman, Roche Bioscience, Siemens, Sun Microsystems, Toyota, U.S. Postal Service, United Way, USAA, Verizon, The Walt Disney Company, and VISA.

Jim Kouzes is an Executive Fellow at the Center for Innovation and Entrepreneurship at the Leavey School of Business, Santa Clara University, California. He is also the chairman emeritus of the Tom Peters Company, a professional services firm specializing in leadership development. Jim is featured as one of the workplace experts in *What Works at Work: Lessons from the Masters* (1988) and in *Learning Journeys: Top Management Experts Share Hard-Earned Lessons on Becoming Great Mentors and Leaders*. Not only is he a highly regarded leadership scholar and an experienced executive, but he was also cited in the *Wall Street Journal* as one of the twelve most requested nonuniversity executive education providers to U.S. companies. A popular seminar and conference speaker, Jim shares his insights about the leadership practices that contribute to high performance in individuals and organizations, and he leaves his audiences inspired with practical leadership tools and tips that they can apply at work, at home, and in their communities. Jim can be reached at jim@kouzesposner.com.

Barry Posner, Ph.D., is dean of the Leavey School of Business and professor of leadership at Santa Clara University, California, where he has received numerous teaching and innovation awards, including his school's and his university's highest faculty awards. An internationally renowned scholar and educator, Barry is the author or coauthor of more than one hundred research and practitioner-focused articles in such publications as *Academy of Management Journal, Journal of Applied Psychology, Human Relations, Personnel Psychology, IEEE Transaction on Engineering Management, Journal of Business Ethics, California Management Review,* and *Business Horizons*. Barry is on the editorial review boards for the *Journal of Business Ethics* and *Leadership Review*. Having consulted with a wide variety of public- and private-sector organizations around the globe, Barry currently sits on the Board of Trustees for the San Jose Repertory Theatre and the Board of Directors for Advanced Energy (NASDAQ:AEIS). He has served previously on the Board for the American Institute of Architects (AIA), Public Allies, Big Brothers/Big Sisters of Santa Clara County, Junior Achievement of Silicon Valley and Monterey Bay, The Center for Excellence in Non-Profits, Sigma Phi Epsilon Fraternity, and several start-up companies. Barry can be reached at bposner@scu.edu.

More information about Jim Kouzes and Barry Posner and their work can be found at their website: www.theleadershipchallenge.com.

Want to continue developing your leadership skills?

Take advantage of The Student Leadership Planner

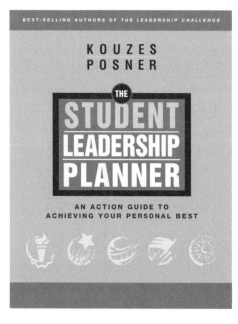

The Planner is designed to be a step-by-step guide to help you effectively use The Five Practices of Exemplary Student Leadership® to continue meeting your leadership challenges. The Planner can enhance your personal leadership development and capabilities.

Now that you've taken the first step in becoming a better leader by completing the *Student Leadership Practices Inventory*, keep moving ahead. *The Student Leadership Planner* picks up where the Workbook leaves off. . . . with Action Plans! Did you do what you said you would do? What did you learn and how can you apply these lessons to future challenges?

The Student Leadership Planner will enable students to continue growing and developing themselves as leaders on their own.